European]

This is the sixth installment of a monthly series on European fairy tales.

Subscribe via Patreon to receive an e-booklet in PDF every month.

More info at:

www.carolynemerick.com/books

Subscribe at:

www.patreon.com/carolynemerick

Table of Contents

1 Introduction   5

2 The Early Slavs to the Western Slavs   10

3 *Dvoeverie* – Slavic Double Faith   17

4 What We Know About Slavic Mythology   25

5 The German Cultural Connection   36

6 Analysis of the German Variant   42

7 Norse Myth and Otherworld Journeys   56

8 Baba Yaga as Ancient Goddess   71

9 Slavic Mythical Elements   78

10 "The Three Golden Hairs"   84

   Bibliography   123

Baba Yaga's hut, by Ivan Bilibin

1

Introduction

This is the first book in the Fairy Tales Series to venture into Slavic culture. The tale we'll be looking at comes from Czech oral tradition, but like most fairy tales, it has variants found elsewhere in Europe. What can be interesting in looking at fairy tale variants is that we can see how a story travels, how certain structural elements remain the same, but details and particulars can vary to suit the specific culture.

When we look at different linguistic-cultural groups throughout Europe, relatedness is of course most readily spotted within closely related language groups. For example, the linguistic relationship between Odin, Woden, and Wotan makes ties between Norse, Anglo-Saxon, and German mythology quite obvious. But, when we shift into languages that are more widely separated from one another, Germanic to Slavonic for example, names and words often don't reveal immediate connections to the non-specialist.

However, the vast majority of European culture groups descend from a shared linguistic origin, Proto-Indo-European language spoken by the ancient Aryans. The Aryan migration and influence on European mythos was discussed in Volume IV of this series (The Star Money), so we won't go into too much detail here. But it is relevant to spend a moment on language/culture splits.

It is believed that the Aryans originated in Central Asia and then spread out in virtually all directions over a period stretching from 4,000-1,000 BC. The two main branches are known today as the Indo-Europeans and the Indo-Iranians. Modern European language and mythos has a very ancient tie to Sanskrit and to Indian Hinduism. As explained in Vol. IV, the idea that Europeans stem from a "Judeo-Christian" worldview is very misleading, and that concept is quite recent in the

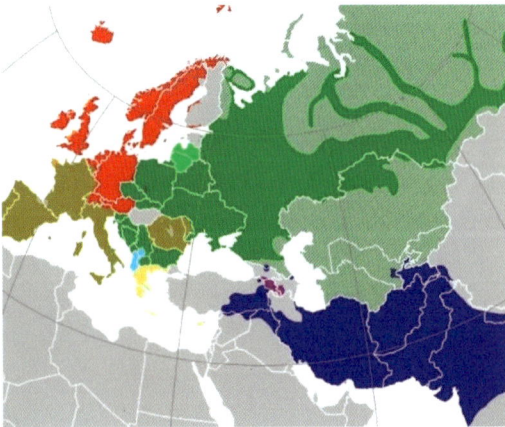

Map of Indo-European Languages

grand scheme of the history and development of European culture.

Biblical myth was born out of Semitic linguistic-mythos, which does not fall on the Indo-European language family tree. In fact, the worldview outlined within the Hebrew Bible was so foreign to Europeans that a great deal of adaptation had to be applied in order to make Christianity appealing to Europeans. But, as we continue to see demonstrated repeatedly in the folk tradition, the idea that Europeans collectively one day just shed their native faith for the foreign one is preposterous. Indigenous folkways lived on into the modern era.

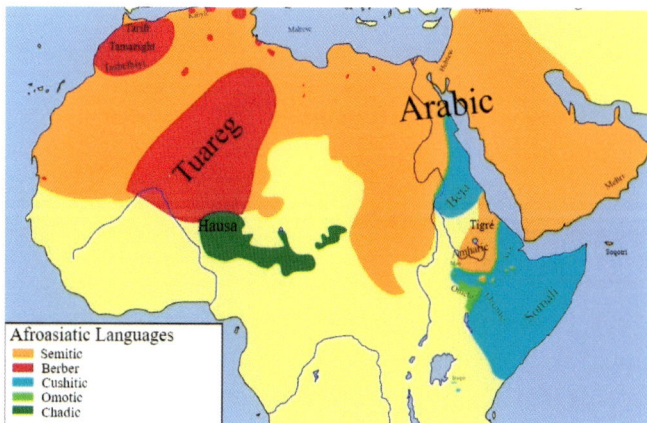

Map of Semitic and other Afro-Asiatic Languages

Returning to European cultural origins, as the Indo-European Aryans continued to spread out and populate ever wider territories, eventually their languages began to differ and separate into "proto" languages. These are precursors to the language families we're familiar with today. For example, Old English, Old German, and Old Norse all developed from proto-Germanic language.

A more recent analogy that most people are familiar with are the Romance languages. In exactly the same way, more recently in time, the Roman Empire spread out and its culture fully dominated some of its neighbors to the degree that their native languages were lost and they became linguistically saturated by Latin (which is also another Indo-European language). In time, these language groups began to separate from one another and form distinct languages we know today as French, Spanish, and Italian.

So, while language is wont to separate, shift, form dialects, and evolve, certain threads of continuity remain among language speakers who stem from a shared origin. We can still see the interrelatedness of Indo-European languages in words that are very primal and universally basic, such as family pronouns. Please see the chart on the following page.

Modern English	Gothic	Latin	Sanskrit	Old Slavonic
mother	móðir	māter	mātár	mati, mater
brother	brōþar	frāter	bʰrā́tar	bratrŭ
sister	swistar	soror	svásar	sestra
daughter	daúhtar	futír	duhitár	dŭšti, dŭšter

Language and mythos are tied together. Throughout the vast majority of human history, a cultural identity was comprised of a fusion of ethnicity, language, and mythos. There was no real concept of "religion" to peoples practicing their native faith, for all intuitive and organic spiritual paths had always been intertwined with culture, language, and ethnic identity. In other words, our myths were as much a part of us as the language we spoke, and as deeply important to us as our ancestral inheritance.

This is relevant as it helps us understand the mythic situation among the Slavic peoples as we will explore both how their languages developed and how Christianity was imposed upon them in ways that differ slightly from other Indo-European culture groups.

2

The Early Slavs to the Western Slavs

The Slavic peoples have a somewhat unique cultural experience compared to some other European language groups. Scholars believe that the earliest Slavs were one singular and identifiable ethnic group. But that cannot be said of modern Slavic people, which is comprised of a plethora of distinct ethnic groups related by shared mytho-linguistic heritage.

The Slavs are believed to have had their origins in a wide range that covers what is now eastern Poland, Ukraine, Belarus, and western Russia. In about the year 150 AD, Slavic groups began expanding into wider territory. Eventually, these groups would split into three main linguistic groups:

East Slavic	West Slavic	South Slavic
Russian	Polish	Slovenian
Belorussian	Czech	Serbo-Croation
Ukranian	Slovak	Macedonian
		Bulgarian

Although the Slavonic languages did split into separate (but still closely related) families, scholars believe that these splits occurred more slowly than in other European language families. In other words, the Slavonic language remained more tightly related in a singular form, perhaps shifting into dialects but not distinct languages, for a longer period of time than the various branches of other linguistic families (such as German, Celtic, etc).

As we have mentioned, language, ethnicity, and mythos had always been very closely linked within a given culture when said culture was operating under its indigenous worldview. Therefore, it seems that a slower separation between the Slavonic language family allowed for the Slavic cultural mythos to remain even more strongly embedded in the Slavic consciousness in a unified way, even across wide distances, and even when Slavic culture came to absorb different ethnic groups.

Slavic language distribution

Shifting to focus specifically on the Western Slavs, as our story for this volume is a Czech tale, we can see that both the conversion process, as well as interactions with their closest neighbors, played a role in West Slavic folk tradition.

When and how a culture is converted to a foreign ideology often impacts how the indigenous beliefs survive within a particular ethnic group. The Western Slavs' closest non-Slavic neighbors were the Germans to the west and the Magyars (Hungarians) to the east. The Germans were largely forcibly converted under Charlemagne, and the bloody story of his massacre of the Saxons in the name of the Christian religion is one of the goriest in European history. The forced conversion of the Germans effectively resulted in transforming them into conquistadors and crusaders. Armies from Charlemagne's troops to the later Teutonic Knights were sent out into their neighboring lands on convert or die campaigns.

The modern Czech Republic and its closely related neighbor, Slovakia, are largely comprised of what were known in ancient times through the High Middle Ages as the kingdoms of Moravia and Bohemia. We know that the region was an active trading center and the West Slavs in this area became so wealthy that Charlemagne forbade the trading of arms with them.

By the 10th century AD, German armies had continued to push westward in efforts to convert the still pagan Slavs. Several West Slavic tribes located near German lands (largely what is Poland today) were collectively referred to as the "Wends" by the Christian German chroniclers. These campaigns were successful to a degree for some time. But, in the year 982, Germans under Otto II were defeated by Arabs in a battle that occurred hundreds of miles away from their homeland. Seeing their weakened state as an opportunity to attack, the Wends launched an uprising. They pushed the Germans back all the way to the city of Hamburg, which they burned and looted. By shaking off German control, the Wends returned to their native faith.

Pagan Slavs practicing their religion

The author of "The Barbarian Conversion from Paganism to Christianity," Richard Fletcher, points out that this is a very close parallel to an earlier pagan Saxon uprising against their Christian Frankish oppressors that had occurred approximately 200 years prior. So, we can clearly see that the conversion of both the Germans and the Slavs was not a painless process, and that the tribes of Central Europe did not give up their native faith, quite literally, without a fight.

Bishop Absalon topples the god Svantevit at Arkona by Laurits Tuxen

The Wends' close neighbors to the south, the Bohemians, converted somewhat differently. In the 9th Century, the Western Slavs in what is now the Czech Republic found themselves enduring attacks by the Magyars to the east which spurred Bohemian chieftains to seek help from their German neighbors. The deal was conversion in exchange for protection.

Conversion for political reasons is the other main mode of conversion seen in Northern (by that I mean non-Greco-Latin, non-Mediterranean) Europe in addition to conversion through military campaigns. A king or chieftain is often seen converting as a political maneuver to gain some advantage, as seen here with the Bohemians, or by marrying a Christian princess to create an alliance with a strong Christian nation. In this case, sometimes the converted king will be the one using terror to force conversion upon his own people, such as was seen by King Olaf of Norway in the year 995.

Whether the conversion comes from an outside aggressor or a nation's own leader, the common peasants are typically slow to receive the memo. What this means is that a country will be said to have converted at a certain date in the history books, but it could take decades to centuries for the new religion to saturate amongst the peasantry. And more often than not, the new religion was superimposed over their way of life as a veneer, while the age old indigenous beliefs and practices continued to carry right on among the populace. This is true clear across Europe, but especially so amongst the Slavic peoples.

Modern Slavic pagans practicing their religion in Russia in the year 2000

3

Dvoeverie – Slavic Double Faith

I argue quite strongly that the phenomenon of holding a hybrid form of religion occurred clear across Northern Europe, from Britain clear to Russia. However, the manifestation of it occurred much more strongly in Slavic lands than elsewhere. In fact, the ancient faith of the Slavs was so overtly prominently practiced by the peasantry that the Slavs began to be referred to as the people of two faiths. *Dvoeverie* is a Russian word that is typically translated as "dual belief" or "double faith."

Modern Russians burning pagan effigy. Photo by Vladimir Lobachev

17

Unfortunately for English speakers interested in Slavic groups other than Russian, the vast bulk of material available in English only covers Russian culture, especially as it pertains to mythology and folklore. However, as mentioned above, the slow nature of the separation of Slavonic languages means that Slavic mythology likely retained a strong continuity between various Slavic language speakers. Therefore, studying scholarship on Russian folklore will still help us understand lore and practices of other Slavic groups.

There are other similarities between the different Slavic groups that allowed them to remain both closely related and tied closely to their indigenous folkways. One important factor is that most of the Slavic lands remained quite rural and agrarian based, so they were less abruptly affected by the kind of urbanization elicited by the Industrial Revolution in the West. In addition, the Slavic nations remained strongly Orthodox in the East and Catholic in the West (Poland, Bohemia), and so they were not affected by the purge on native practices that was brought with the Protestant Reformation in the West. It is also worth mentioning that the Renaissance was a decidedly Western phenomenon. So, we can see that most of the Slavic people were insulated from several movements that shook things up in Western Europe.

We are so removed from these events today that we may not immediately understand their cultural ramifications. Urbanization drastically reduced the rural peasant population in Western nations, which had an eroding effect on the preservation of rural folk customs. Prior to that, the Protestant Reformation attacked not only Roman Catholicism, but also all of the indigenous European beliefs and practices that had been allowed to continue to flourish under the Catholic Church. While native European belief did certainly live on after those events, it certainly took quite a hit by both social movements.

Lastly, the role that the U.S.S.R. played in preserving Slavic culture also must be emphasized. Much has been said about communist attacks on religion, how it promoted atheism, and pushed homogenized thought upon its people. This is all true. However, the other thing that Soviet rule did is wall the Slavs off from Western cultural influence. Without foreign mass media breaking through to lure people away from their culture, the Soviet Union essentially placed Slavic people in a time capsule for several decades.

While religion was frowned upon under Soviet rule, nationalism was encouraged. Fairy and folk tales seemed innocuous enough to communist leaders, so they were not suppressed in the same way that Christianity was. In fact, fairy and folk

Russian Fairy Tale Art by Yelena Polenova

tales served as a vehicle by which Russian and other Slavic writers and artists could express themselves during an age when self-expression was severely limited. So, therefore, the magical realm of fairy tales and folklore continued to flourish and inspire ballets, film, artwork, and literature.

The period when this double faith was especially noted was during the period of folklore collecting in the late 19th century. The field of folklore boomed throughout Europe at this time. Though there had been some examples of earlier collecting of folk belief in the West, there was no field of study dedicated to it until the Romantic Era of the 19th century influenced a boom of interest in folk tradition and European native culture. The folklore craze moved into Russia a little later than elsewhere, but soon enough folklorists could be found in the field collecting peasants' tales in the same way that the Grimm brothers had done in Germany.

It has been noted that virtually every ethnographic study of Russian peasant belief made a point to acknowledge the strong presence of paganism in the daily life and beliefs of the common folk. One researcher commented that one thousand years of Christianity had only penetrated the Slavic consciousness superficially, while their indigenous paganism comprised the deep roots of Slavic daily life and belief. Yet another researcher

21

found himself recording folklore from a rural Russian fellow who claimed to have never before heard of Jesus Christ! The notes record that he had heard something about God from his parents but, no, nothing about Christ. What this demonstrates is that in very remote and rural areas of Russia into the late 19th and probably early 20th century, there were still peasants who had never been converted to Christianity and were still practicing a form of native faith. And in fact, we know that there *are* still some groups in Russia today who still have not converted, most notably the Mari El people, known as "Europe's last pagans."

That example is extreme, and it does not seem to speak for the majority of Slavic peasants. But, it is worth noting as it speaks to how much more slowly belief changes trickled out into the vast remote areas in Slavic lands as opposed to the smaller and more urban-industrialized Western nations. And, researchers who noted that their Slavic subjects did attend church regularly made sure to note that their research subjects were Christian on Sundays but returned to their pagan ways as soon as they returned home.

In addition to belief about nature spirits, rituals (sometimes lingering as superstitions), tales, and other ways that native belief carried on among the peasantry, a great deal of pagan imagery remained a constant within Slavic folk art. Images and symbols traced back to ancient pagan gods are still common motifs in Slavic folk crafts.

The phenomenon of pagan deities being transformed into Christian saints is observed clear across Europe. But, as mentioned above, the Slavs did not experience a Protestant Reformation to wash away their cult of saints. So whether Catholic or Orthodox, the pantheon of Christian saints was yet one more way in which the attributes of pagan deities could carry on in the Slavic folk consciousness in a way that died off in northwestern Protestant Europe.

One point that speaks volumes is that when scholars look at recorded sermons from the time of conversion to Christianity (roughly the 10th century, varying by locale) and then compare them to the notes made by ethnographers recording folk traditions in the late 19th and early 20th century, they find many of the exact same practices that Christian priests rallied against at the pulpit were still being practiced by Slavic peasants a good millennium later.

In some of my other work, I have pointed out that one source of information to understand native European practices that have since died out is to look at church sermons, papal bulls and edicts, and other Church communications written closely to the time of conversion. In my article, "The Hidden History of Christmas Carols," I mentioned that one piece of evidence for the tradition of Christmas caroling having a pagan origin (although only Christian carols survive today) is that there is written documentation very close to the period of the conversion of the Anglo-Saxons that rallies against the practice, and that the Church actually tried to ban it. So that certain practices described in Church sermons from the point of nominal conversion were still being practiced by Slavic peasants a good one thousand years later speaks volumes about the notion of a living dual-faith that carried on unbroken.

Czech fairy tale illustration by Jan Matulka

4

What We Know About Slavic Mythology

It is often said that our knowledge of Teutonic mythology is patchy compared to the breadth of information preserved on the Greco-Roman tradition. Unfortunately, the situation is much worse for Slavic myth. For a variety of reasons, sources describing the complete pantheon of the Slavs, and the exploits of their deities, either did not survive or were never created in the first place. So, we'll take a look at the reasons behind this, at what we do know, and how it can be said that the Slavs remained pagan if we don't actually know what their original pre-Christian religion looked like.

One major obstacle we have is simply the lack of surviving sources. Some scholars say that the Slavs had no writing of their own before St. Cyril invented the Glagolitic script in the 9th century. Some of the characters of the Glagolitic script would later be combined with the Greek alphabet to create the Cyrillic alphabet, possibly created by disciples of Cyril and, hence, named after him. There are some hints in medieval manuscripts leading some scholars to believe that the Slavs did have another writing system prior to Christianization, but if so, no examples survive.

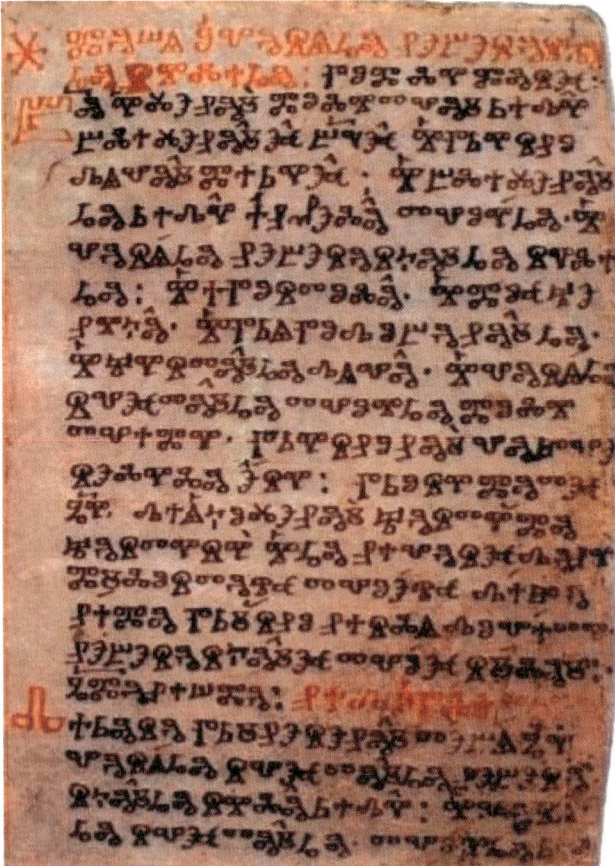

Page from the 10th-century Kiev Missal, an Old Church Slavonic manuscript written in Glagolitic script

The Glagolitic script and later Cyrillic alphabet were invented by Church figures for the express purpose of converting the Slavs. Therefore, it stands to reason that these alphabets would have been known and used predominantly for Church purposes. We do know that the writing material traditionally used by the Slavs was birch bark, due to its availability and paper-like qualities. The inherent problem with birch bark is that it is highly susceptible to decomposition, especially in the cold, damp climates that the Slavs occupied. Not only this, but we know that it was common for Church officials to collect and destroy pagan artifacts during the conversion period. So, anything that may have been recorded regarding the Slavic gods, whether it was in an unknown indigenous script or a later alphabet, would have been lost to history.

We know that in the case of the Norse and the Celts that Christian monks and scholars made the effort to record the lore of their own people. However, conversion happened a bit differently in both of those cases. The Irish were the first Northern European people to have converted. They seem to have also been one of the only Northern European peoples to convert by choice (or at least, no evidence of coercion survives in the record. Caesar's slaying of the druids was political, not religious, and Rome was not yet Christian at that time). And, being such early converts means that the campaign against their indigenous culture was less aggressive, therefore there was a synthesis of native belief with the new faith still known today as "Celtic Christianity." Thus, learned Irish Catholic monks remained very proud of their own heritage and made the effort to record the legends of their ancestors.

The title page of Olive Bray's English translation of Codex Regius entitled Poetic Edda depicting the tree Yggdrasil and a number of its inhabitants by W. G. Collingwood.

In the case of the Norse, much of what we know we owe to an Icelandic scholar by the name of Snorri Sturluson. Iceland's conversion, like Ireland, seems to be an outlier compared to other Northern European nations. Missionaries had been actively promoting Christianity for several years, and the Icelandic king, Olaf Tryggvason, ascended the throne shortly after having converted himself. As is often the case, Iceland faced political pressure from allies; most especially from Norway in this case. But, rather than a bloody forced conversion of his own people, such as Norway's conversion under their king, Olaf Haraldsson, Olaf Tryggvason called a meeting to discuss the matter among his community. It is said that the "law-speaker" who had the final decision was actually a pagan who weighed the pros and cons and announced that Iceland should convert.

It may be that since the decision was made in such an unusually fair manner, coupled with Iceland's position as an island quite separated from the goings on in mainland Europe (Ireland was also in this position), that there was not quite the same level of crackdown on native folkways of the Icelanders. So this allowed for a climate where an individual would find value in writing down the old lore of his countrymen.

The case for the Slavic people seems more typical of the type of conversion seen in mainland

Europe. Different Slavic nations converted at different times and in different ways. But, as explained in Chapter 2, several Slavic groups were subjected to violent conversion campaigns, particularly the Western Slavs known as the Wends.

In the case of Bohemia, as discussed in Chapter 2, conversion occurred for political purposes in order to gain their German neighbors as an ally against the invading Magyars around the end of the 9th Century. This more or less handed religious authority over to German churchmen. It is recorded that of the first Christian bishops in Bohemia, four out of five were German.

The Christianization of the Poles by Jana Matejki

Compared to Ireland and Iceland where conversion was more self-directed and casual (if you will), one can see where there would be more freedom to write down and preserve native lore in those environments as opposed to one where pious (more likely zealot) Church leaders came from a neighboring nation. In the second scenario, the Church leaders would be looking at the local native beliefs, which would be foreign to them, with disdain.

Ironically, the best roster we have of a confirmed Slavic pantheon comes from a Russian ruler who would later be remembered as a saint in numerous Christian denominations. King Vladimir the Great ruled the Kieven Rus from the end of the 10th century to the early 11th. Like some other famous Slavic leaders called Vladimir who came later in history, this Vlad seems like quite an eccentric fellow. He clearly had a personal fascination with religion. It seems that he initially took pride in his native faith, as when he ascended to the throne, he erected great monuments to several Slavic pagan deities. Medieval chronicles from the period record that there were six statues in all. The figures were wooden, but their heads were adorned with gold and silver. Thanks to the chroniclers, we know that six particular deities were thought important enough to be included; *Perun, Khors, Dazhbog, Stribog, Simargl,* and only one female, *Mokosh*.

A modern statue of Mokosh in a Czech forest. Photo by Wikimedia user: Mido mokomido

Vladimir the Great was, apparently, being courted by emissaries from several religions which represented strong alliances in neighboring areas. The story goes that he sent representatives around to investigate all the great religions of neighboring regions and report back. The German Christians seemed quite dull. Islam was ruled out due to their prohibition of pork and alcohol. It is said that Vladimir scoffed and exclaimed that the Rus loved drinking far too much to ever give it up. But, when his representatives returned from Constantinople, they professed such awe of the splendor that they witnessed in the Eastern Orthodox churches and the beauty of their ceremony that Vladimir was convinced to convert his people to the Eastern Orthodox faith. Subsequently, all six idols were toppled over and dumped in the nearby river.

One might be scratching their head and wondering if this is our only roster of Slavic gods and no actual myths survive at all, how can it be said that paganism lived on among the Slavic people? And, this is an excellent question, for the answer demonstrates the very theory which is the focus of this entire series: the faith of the people lived on in the folk tradition.

Archetypal variants of the old indigenous deities continued to live on in folk and fairy tales. Peasants continued to believe in spirits of the land and of the household. Rituals and practices that accompanied these beliefs continued to be practiced. In a way, it's very ironic that researchers have proclaimed the Slavs to have retained their indigenous faith more profoundly than other Europeans when hardly any shred of their early belief was recorded for posterity. But, that also speaks to the profound power that indigenous faith has over the psyche of a culture and the nature of collective cultural unconscious.

Linguists, philographers, ethnographers, and folklorists have been able to pair the scraps from the documentary record with the oral folk tradition and piece together a Slavic pantheon. Linguists spend lifetimes reconstructing missing elements of language, and thus, also reconstruct the names of lost deities. Words that developed from an age old connection to pagan deities can give clues to the presence and attributes of the old gods. Through folktales, we can often ascertain which archetypal figures match Slavic deities and what attributes were associated with them. And, of course, archeology constantly sheds light on the lives of our ancient ancestors.

So, in essence, a solid written account would make things much easier for researchers. But, the absence of such documentary evidence does not mean that we have nothing to go on. And, in the case of the Slavic people, the very lives of the peasants living right on up into very recent times, indeed even living today in some areas, are a testament to the beliefs of their ancestors. In this short volume, we don't have time to explore the breadth of Slavic mythology. So, in the next chapters we will explore what we find in the Czech fairy tale we're going to be looking at.

Modern Slavic pagans worshiping at a statue of Perun in Ukraine. Photo by Boryslav Javir.

5

The German Cultural Connection

"The Three Golden Hairs" is an especially interesting tale to represent the first appearance of Slavic culture in this series. It evidences the strong mythic thread that bonds all Slavonic language speakers together. Yet, because of the cultural overlap that Western Slavs share with their German neighbors, there is evidence of a continuity between Central European people irrespective of language family. In fact, there are several figures prominent in Alpine and wider Central European culture from Northern Italy through Switzerland/Austria, on to Germany, Poland, and Czech Republic, one of which may be echoed in this tale, as we shall see.

That this tale demonstrates a relationship with both German and Slavic culture is one element that makes it a decidedly "Czech" tale. It was mentioned Chapter 4 that the conversion of Bohemia involved a strong German hand in exchange for German protection against invading Magyars. In the High Middle Ages, large numbers of Germans were invited to settle in Bohemia for their in-demand skills and artistry.

For several hundred years, nearly a millennium, whole communities of Germans could be found in Czech and Slovak regions, and, indeed, throughout Central and Eastern Europe. In the Czech and Slovak (Bohemian) regions they were known as the Carpathian Germans, Sudeten Germans, and Zipser Saxons. At one point in time, ethnic-Germans made up as much as 23% of the Czech population. Sadly, ethnic-cleansing beginning in the mid-19th century and reaching a zenith after WWII has virtually erased the ethnic-German presence from this region. However, folklore remains as a testament of the relationship that the Bohemian culture once nurtured between Western Slavic and German ethnic groups.

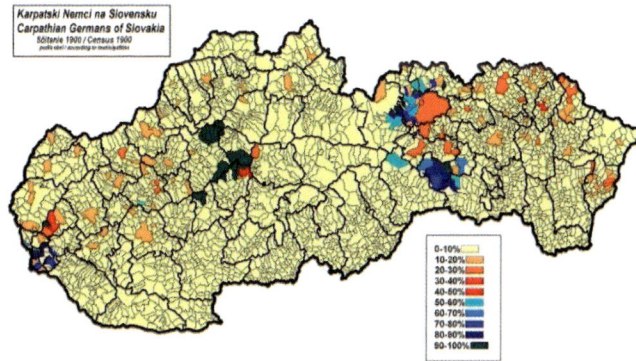

Carpathian Germans in Slovakia in 1900

As mentioned above, the bulk of scholarly analysis on Slavic folklore available in English is largely centered on Russian culture. "The Oxford Companion to Fairy Tales," edited by Jack Zipes, includes a lengthy essay on Slavic fairy tales. But, it hardly mentions Czechoslovak tradition at all. Interestingly, the first thing mentioned is that of all the Slavic nations, Czech folklore is influenced by German culture more than any other. The only other insight it gives us is that Slovak folklore is very similar to Czech, but with a slightly different national flavor, and that a characteristic feature that appears frequently in Czechoslovak tales is the figure of a cunning servant who uses his intellect to outwit adversaries. Interestingly, that figure is commonly found in German folklore as well.

There are actually quite a number of figures that overlap between Germanic and Slavic mythology that lingered on in the folk tradition of both language groups. The maternal domestic goddess figure, often represented with distaff or spinning wheel, is seen in the goddesses Frigga (Norse), Holle (German), and Mokosh (Slavic). We're going to discuss the concept of the "spinning goddess" in a future volume in this series. And, it does relate to the maternal fairy godmother figure that we discussed in Volume V. In both German and Slavic folklore, this maternal goddess figure often appears in elderly form. The German goddess Holle remains in her own fairy tale as well as other folk memories. And, the Slavic Baba Yaga seems to have a strong parallel when she appears in her kindly aspect, which we will explore further in the following chapter.

Modern statue of Frau Holle in Germany. Photo by Markus Goebel

Other mythical parallels between Germanic and Slavic mythology are seen in deities such as *Thor* (Norse), *Donar* (German), and *Perun* (Slavic). This figure also has a parallel in the Baltic deity, *Perkunas*. All four groups placed a high status on the "Thunderer." In both Germanic languages and Baltic, the god's name is also the word for thunder. It is believed that Baltic Perkunas and Slavic Perun both stem from the same Proto-Indo-European deity, *Perkwunos*. It is very interesting that it is believed that the root word is the PIE *perkwu*, which meant "oak." In all of these cultures, the Thunder God is associated with oak trees. It is very strongly documented that Germanic tribes worshiped Donar at oak trees in sacred groves. These connections speak to the ancient shared origins of these mytho-linguistic cultures before their divergence and separation.

But, there are other ties that appear much more recent, especially between the Western Slavs and the Germans, which are indicative of cultural diffusion through geographic proximity and interaction. For example, the German Christmas season is famous for monstrous figures like Krampus and Percht. These are complex figures that could fill entire chapters in their own right, but suffice to say that they are depicted as hairy, beastly, frightening characters who terrorize the children of the villages at the winter solstice time. Interestingly, similar figures can be seen throughout the Alpine region even into northern Italy to the south, stretching up through Central Europe into Poland in the northeast. This speaks to a continuity of folk culture in Central Europe that transcends language barriers and national boundaries.

Perun by M. Presnyakov

6

Analysis of the German Variant

"The Three Golden Hairs" is interesting because this Czech tale has a German variant that shows strong a structural parallel but stark differences in the rendering. Both stories feature a poor peasant boy blessed in infancy to achieve a great destiny; marrying the king's daughter. They both feature a vindictive king who tries to thwart this young man's destiny both in his infancy and again upon adulthood. In both stories, the child escapes death and the young man overcomes obstacles with supernatural assistance to achieve his destiny.

The German version, found in the Grimms' collection, contains evidence of pagan belief and subsequent superstition, but in a much more muted way. It says that this child was born with the caul, and that is why he was singled out for this great destiny. The "caul" is a piece amniotic membrane that can sometimes cover an infant at birth. In even rarer cases, an infant may be born fully encased by the membrane. Cases of being born with a caul are estimated to be only one in 80,000 births. Because of the rarity of this occurrence, it became steeped in superstition and children born with a caul were attributed various connotations over the years. In some cultures it was a sign that the child would have shamanic ability, in others it was a sign of good fortune. Belief in the auspiciousness of the caul lived on well into the turn of the 20th century. So, these beliefs would still have been commonplace at the time that the Grimm brothers were recording and publishing folklore. However, the caul is not present in the Czech version.

Interestingly, the editor of "The Annotated Brother's Grimm," Maria Tatar, seems unaware that this story has a Czech variant. In fairness, the sheer breadth of European folklore means that it's virtually impossible for any scholar to be aware of every folktale, let alone every variant of every folktale. Although, the discipline of folkloristics has created cataloging systems in order organize stories by type and thereby makes finding variants easier once a tale is added to the list. So, why the editor of the "Annotated Grimm" did not know of this version, I can't say. But, it seems a valid point because the existence of the Czech variant causes me to disagree with one of her conclusions.

The presence of the caul in the German version is not the only difference between the two versions of "The Three Golden Hairs." The most

obvious and striking difference is that in the Czech
tale, the protagonist must obtain three golden hairs
from "Grandfather Know-it-all," who turns out to
be a thinly veiled solar deity, whereas in the
German version he must obtain hairs from the devil.
This is quite a significant difference. The Sun is
personified in the Czech tale, and is presented with
his own mother who appears to be an aspect of
Baba Yaga in her kindly, grandmotherly form. The
editor of the "Annotated Grimm" explains that in
the first publication of Grimms' fairy tales, the
figure of the devil was changed so has not to offend
the sensibilities of the Victorian Era reading public.
So, in the first edition of Grimms' tales, we read
about a hero who must obtain three hairs from a
giant.

Maria Tatar makes an argument in her notes
in the "Annotated Grimm" that she believes that the
original story must have been a giant even though
the Grimms originally recorded it as the devil and
changed it to a giant for sake of public relations.
She compares the tale to "Jack in the Beanstalk" as
evidence of an earlier root for a common giant tale.
Well, I did a lot of digging to research this tale. It
was only in searching through additional Slavic
folktale collections that I came upon a note
indicating that this tale even had a German variant.
And in searching for information on the German
version, I found some interesting tidbits of

information. That plus comparative analysis leads me to a different conclusion.

*An early edition of The Brothers' Grimm
Children and Household Tales*

That the Czech version features a personified Sun as the figure that the German version calls the devil (and/or a giant), in my view, is very telling. Personification of elements and cosmological forces is a very primal characteristic in the mythic tradition. As explained earlier in this chapter, the example of "the Thunderer" as an important mythic archetype is universal in Indo-European mythology. And, that is only one such example. In studying Slavic folklore, it very quickly becomes clear that elemental, cosmological, and earthy personifications are rife in the Slavic consciousness.

Mokosh appears frequently in Russian folk art. This pattern appears on a cloth from the 19th century.

We discussed already how although we don't have the original Slavic myths preserved, that we can still very plainly see ancient mythic elements overtly in Slavic folklore. One personification not seen in this tale, but that which makes a great analogy and which is very common in the Slavic folk tradition, is known as "Damp Mother Earth." In Slavonic languages she is called *Mat Zemlya, Matka Ziemia,* and *Mati Syra Zemlya.* "Damp Mother Earth" is a literal translation. Her presence is so pervasive that scholars believe she is perhaps the oldest known Slavic deity. And, as we mentioned that pagan beliefs and practices lingered on very strongly even into the modern era, it is worth noting that several practices pertaining to this figure have been observed among Slavic peasants. In some places, when making oaths of great and binding significance, the oath takers swallowed a handful of earth (dirt) to sanctify their promise. In other cases, it has been recorded that if a Christian priest could not be found to give a final confession to, that Slavic peasants gave confession to Mother Earth on their deathbed.

With this background information, we know that the presence of an anthropomorphic sun character in a Slavic folk tale is no arbitrary coincidence. In fact, the sun did have great importance to the Slavs, and there is striking evidence that the Czech version is an overt representation of a solar deity, which we will discuss further in the next chapter.

It can be difficult to know if a folktale came from one culture and traveled into another, vice versa, or if the variants developed from a common source and drifted apart. Tales are wont to change to suit the culture they find themselves in. And, just like myths, they can split and diverge, they can also be influenced by other tales and be changed, and two tales might end up merged into one.

But, in this case, my guess is that the tale either originated with the Slavs and moved to German speaking realms, or they originated from the same source and evolved separately. In either scenario, it appears that the Czech version remained closer to the earlier form. I do not believe it is possible that it originated in German and moved eastward to Slavic lands, *unless* it came to Bohemia with very *early* German settlers still telling it an older version, then spread among the Czechs and was preserved in that form there while it later evolved independently in Germany (this occurrence is seen in certain folk traditions that traveled to America and were preserved among European descendants in the U.S. while the original folkway died out in the homeland). In any case, however it happened, it seems that the Czech tale preserves elements that have been lost in the German version.

As explained in previous chapters, the Germans were converted earlier than the Bohemians (Czechs/Slovaks), and they practiced a stricter form of Christianity than the Slavs. This is not to say that there is typically less paganism found in German folklore in general. As we saw in Vol V of this series, often there is very overt pagan influence found in the tales recorded by the Grimms. However, there are many factors that can influence the evolution of a folktale, from the social climate of the specific village it is being told in, to the beliefs and ideas of the storyteller telling it. So, while we do have very strong remnants in many German folktales, this particular one seems to have met with alterations wrought by religious sensibilities as it traveled through Germany.

Between all neighboring people there was always cultural interchange. So, folktales certainly could have, and very likely did, travel between these two neighboring groups; especially as there were German speaking communities in the Czechoslovak region. However, the nature of the evolution of folklore is that it evolves to appease the new religion, it does not devolve backwards into old mythological belief.

In other words, the presence of pagan mythical elements are evidence of their hanging on despite religious upheaval, but their true meaning is often lost on the people telling the story due to such a great disparity in the timeline between the origins and the retelling under an altered religious climate. Therefore, the logical progression of the evolution of a folktale is that a pagan god is often demonized and replaced in the tale as a "devil." But, it is never the case that a folktale featuring a devil would travel to a new location, where the people are also Christian, and be transformed back into a pagan deity.

Depiction of the devil as seen in the medieval manuscript, the Codex Gigas.

50

We have discussed that the Slavs kept their pagan beliefs alive to the degree that their worldview has been called a "double faith." This is simply an extreme version of what is known as "popular religion;" which is a hybrid of indigenous beliefs with the new faith. Although hybridization occurs, there is generally not an awareness in the consciousness of the people that they are, in fact, practicing a dual faith. They typically hold a self-identity as Christian without any conception that half of their practices are of pagan origin. It is simply their native way of life and they don't stop to analyze it.

So whether this tale moved from Bohemia into Germany and then was altered, came in to Bohemia in an earlier form from Germany, became known to the Czechs and then was later altered in Germany, or whether the two versions are sourced from the same root and evolved independently is difficult to know. However, the fact that the same figure is depicted as the personified Sun in the Czech version and the Devil in the German version speaks to the veracity of the Czech version as being closer to the source of origin for the simple reason that in the evolution of folklore, a pagan deity is likely to be transformed into a devil under a strict Christian climate, but a devil is very unlikely to transform back into a pagan deity if the population has been remotely Christianized.

But, this brings us to another feature in 'The Three Golden Hairs" that bonds these two cultures together. It was mentioned above that maternal goddess figures are found fairly universally in Indo-European mythology and subsequently within the fairy tale tradition. We explored fairy godmothers as representative of the important role that ancestral female spirits played in Teutonic mythic consciousness in Vol. V of this series. Above, the concept of spinning goddesses was briefly touched on, and how they are pervasive in folklore clear across Europe (to be explored in a future volume). Well "The Three Golden Hairs" features a fairy godmother who assists the male protagonist upon his journey. We'll go deeper into the mythology behind it within the Czech version in the following chapter. But, in searching for more insight on this tale, I found something very interesting regarding the characterization present in the German variant as well.

As we're going to see in the story, this Czech fairy tale features an anthropmorphic sun figure. The three golden hairs of the Sun are the item that the hero must retrieve in order to secure his destiny. The hero's fairy godmother, it turns out, is also the mother of the Sun. In the German version, she is the grandmother of the devil. Well, it turns out that "the devil's grandmother" is a folk figure who turns up frequently in the German folk tradition.

Luckily enough, I was able to track down an article in the "Journal of American Folklore" from the year 1900 that discusses "the devil's grandmother" as a character who features in German folk consciousness. The article, titled "The Devil's Grandmother," by Isobel Cushman Chamberlain, says that:

Of all peoples, the Teutons, the modern Low Germans especially, seem to have had the most kindly feeling towards the devil, furnishing him at times with a wife, a mother, and a grandmother, the last, who is often indistinguishable from the second, being the most important and interesting character.

She mentions that there is no Biblical record of the devil having any genealogy, but somehow this appears in the European folklore, which is curious. Chamberlain points out that even Shakespeare mentioned "the devil and his dam." The author goes on to give quite a lengthy list of phrases that include the devil and his grandmother that were at one time common among German peasants. She makes no deep analysis of the origin of this motif, only stating that:

As may be seen from the sayings here recorded, the giants, goblins, and deities of heathen times have helped to color folk-thought about the devil. The devil's mother, or grandmother, often has the popular sympathy, and does not always appear as an evil-doing or as an ugly individual.

Well, I am going to assert that this so called "devil's grandmother" who appears in the Grimms' version of "The Three Golden Hairs" is most certainly a vestigial memory of a goddess, and quite likely a maternal goddess figure. We know that pagan gods were called demons by Church leaders. We know that very important mother goddesses who were once venerated by the European peasantry were demoted and either survived as "fairy godmothers" in fairy tales, or they also were demonized. The German goddess Holle is a great example, for she survived both in her own fairy tale, but is also later associated with the witchy hag archetype, and in addition one aspect of her was transformed into a monstrous and devilish figure known as Perchta.

The appearance of the devil and his grandmother in Grimms' version of "The Three Golden Hairs" is minimal enough where on its own someone might criticize my assertion as mere conjecture. It is when we look deeply into the Czech variant that we see so much more of the pagan origins of the story. After analyzing the Czech version, I do agree with Tatar that this tale has a relationship to "Jack and the Beanstalk." However, I am now inclined to believe that Jack's tale was very likely also very much transformed from its original state by the time it got to the state most of us know it in. But, *that* tangent deserves its own volume in this series! So, we shall move on to the next chapter to look more deeply at the mythology present in the Czech version of this tale.

Bags of gold and silver Jack took
home, but still his mind did lean
Towards another prize, and journey
up the lucky stalk of bean.
Hidden in his usual corner in the
giant's house, he spied,
Bought for that great man's amuse-
ment, playing sweetly by his side
While he slept, a golden harp, which
Jack at once caught up, and ran,
But the harp with human voice cried,
"Master, master, stop this man!"
But so tipsy was the giant, though
he tried to run and bawl,
That, with all his pains, he could not
stop the flight of Jack at all.

Illustration for Jack and the Beanstalk by Walter Crane

7

Norse Myth and Otherworld Journeys

We've touched on and hinted at some mythical elements present in this fairy tale in previous chapters. But, there is so much more to cover, and some of it circles back to discussions we've had in previous volumes of this series.

In Vol. I we discussed the Teutonic Norns, which are analogous to the Greek Moirai, better known as the Fates. These are the three goddesses who are usually depicted with spinning accoutrements which symbolize their role as the weavers and sewers who create our destinies. As with other Indo-European (Aryan) mythical elements which are interwoven throughout the underlying pan-European cultural landscape, there is a thread of continuity found clear across European myth, while retaining unique characteristics within the individual mytho-linguistic groups that they manifest within.

The story of "The Three Golden Hairs" begins with the very typical juxtaposition of royalty against the backdrop of a very poor peasant. The notion of an individual in a denigrated state reaching the zenith of social status is one of the most common storylines within the fairy tale genre. There are discussions to be had on the symbolic meaning of this, such as the individual journey to self-actualization, to be sure. But, as we are focusing on how ancient mythology presents here, we'll move on.

As soon as the story presents this layout that represents the oppositional positions of the high and low end of the social stratum, the first supernatural visitation in the narrative is by the three Fates.

Now, we saw the Fates appear in Vol. I of this series, "The Three Heads of the Well." But, in that story, the figures were vestigial memories rather than overt representations. In other words, the Fates, or more accurately in that case, the Norse (Teutonic) Norns, were depicted in a foggy sort of way where someone without the mythological background knowledge might think they were just some arbitrary fairy tale fantasy characters, (for those who did not read Vol. I, they were depicted as three golden heads floating in a well). It was only through the symbolism and specific verbiage used in the text that it became clear that these figures did, indeed, represent the Norns.

In "The Three Golden Hairs," the narrative describes three supernatural elderly women who appear shortly after the birth of an infant, and one by one they each grant blessings upon the child. This is a common occurrence in European fairy tales. We even see it in Disney's version of "Sleeping Beauty." But, most modern viewers of that film, like most readers of "The Three Heads of the Well," have no idea that three "fairies" (who are, in fact, depicted as granny-ish in the film) giving blessings over the cradle of a child are vestigial memories of the Fates.

Because these appearances are so typically vestigial in nature, i.e. they are faded memories recognizable only to those with the background insight, imagine my surprise to discover that this Czech narrative referred to these three old women directly as "the Fates." The introduction to the initial collection I found the tale in said that the author, Parker Fillmore, had taken some minor artistic liberty to make the tales more readable (as I do, and as all storytellers do), but that he had stayed true to the tales (as I do as well). So, I searched for this story in other folk and fairy tale collections to compare. Fillmore's collection was published in 1919. So, I found a collection of Slavic folktales by A.H. Wratislaw which was published about thirty years prior, in 1890, which also described these women explicitly as "the Fates." At this point, one can only assume that the identification of these figures as "the Fates" is true to how it was rendered by the original Czech oral storytellers. Therefore,

The Fates Gathering in the Stars by Elihu Vedder, 1887

we observe that while Western European fairytales often depict mythical elements as vestigial memories, a bit fuzzy and blurred from their original mythical forms, at least in this instance the Czechs understood very clearly who and what the figures were. So, as discussed previously, again, although we have no recording of ancient Slavic mythology as such, it is very clear that the ancient mythology was very much vividly alive in the Slavic folklore.

The Slavic analogy of the Greek *Moirai* and the Norse *Norns* is the *Sudice*, and the Czech-Slovak variant is the *Sudičky*. And, in this tale, they function precisely as we see the Fates perform in Norse myth, as mentioned in Disney's "Sleeping Beauty," and even Disney's "Hercules." The idea that three old crones stand over an infant's cradle and give gifts that decide his or her fate seems quite universal in the European folk experience.

I can even say that my own grandmother, of pure British stock, swore that she did witness this phenomenon over the cradle of her own firstborn child. You will find that there are unique individual accounts of experiences scattered here and there, even among different language groups, even when living in the New World, and even when the individual was raised strictly Christian, which for no explainable reason jibe with overwhelming continuity to ancient European native faith. In the case of my grandmother, I can assure that she was raised with no pagan inclination whatsoever.

Returning to the tale, as it moves on, we see that one of the Fates also doubles as the hero's fairy godmother. The tale calls her simply "godmother," but as it unfolds, we see that she is clearly otherworldly. Not only is she one of the Fates, but she is also the mother of the solar deity that we're going to meet. The word "fairy" is not used in the narrative, but she certainly is of the realm of *fairy*, i.e. supernatural.

The protagonist of the story, a young man called Plavachek (unnamed in the German version), was blessed with a fortunate destiny at his birth, despite his meager origins and unfortunate circumstances (his mother dies after childbirth). The king of the realm, who is placed at the place of his birth, cannot fathom that this peasant's child is destined to marry his daughter, and becomes Plavachek's nemesis. But, the story very clearly demonstrates that even very powerful enemies cannot thwart what is predetermined by the Fates.

Returning to points noted in previous chapters, despite the lack of written records of ancient myths, we can see already that this Slavic fairy tale bears very overt testimony to the indigenous European worldview that transcends time. For this theme is found in Greek myth dating to Homer's "Illiad" written in the 8th century B.C., again in Norse myth recorded in the Icelandic "Eddas" recorded in the 13th century A.D. These Slavic folktales were collected at the end of the 19th century A.D., and they were collected from uneducated, in many cases even illiterate, peasant folk. Indeed, this speaks to a continuity of indigenous belief that has demonstrably transcended time, religious conversion, and industrial revolution.

Achilles tending the wounded Patroclus, artwork dates to 500 B.C.

But, as the tale moves on, there are several other tidbits of mythology that present themselves. Obviously, as in other tales, this protagonist goes off on what Joseph Campbell described as "the Hero's Journey." His fairy godmother, who is also one of the Fates, blesses and directs him. When his nemesis, the king, sends him on an impossible errand, Plavachek sets out on his quest to prove his worth and secure his birthright. The preposition of the tale sets up his destiny, but then the hero is put in a position where his destiny is wrought away from him and he must prove himself worthy in order to retain it.

When Plavachek sets out, the first figure he encounters the ferryman who steers his boat back and forth across a dark, black sea. The notion of a "ferryman" who brings the dead across the sea to the otherworld is a common motif in European folk belief. To return to the comparison betwixt the Czech and German variations, interestingly the Czech version portrays the hero meeting the ferryman as the *first* of three encounters on his journey, whereas the German story depicts it as the *last* of three. I think this change is significant because of the skewed intention between the two tales.

The ultimate destination of the Czech hero is the palace of "Grandfather Know-it-all" who happens to be the Sun. The final destination of the

German hero is the devil's lair. So therefore, in a Christian context, it makes sense not to present the ferryman until the hero crosses over unto the *Underworld*, or Hell. Anyone who studies indigenous European belief will understand that there is no word "Hell" in the original Greek or Hebrew Biblical texts. The word is strictly Germanic. It was applied, superimposed, or replaced for the concept of the Underworld as described in the Christian New Testament. But, the word itself existed far before the Bible came anywhere near European consciousness in the Teutonic realm called "Hel," one of the nine worlds of Norse cosmology.

Valhalla by Max Brückner

We have to rely a bit on Teutonic and Celtic sources due to the fact that availability of Slavic sources in English are more limited. But, it is certainly fair to say that the Northern European consciousness, which in my view includes Britain clear to Russia, does not draw a delineation between the "Otherworld" and the "Underworld." The realm of the dead and the realm of "fairy" conflate a great deal in Teutonic and Celtic myth and folklore. Again, this is confirmed here in this West Slavic tale.

Just to reiterate, the German folk tradition "in general" does not stick to a pagan or Christian representation, but shifts to "either, or." We discussed in preceding chapters how the conversion process and other social upheavals can play a huge role in folk consciousness. The Germans were by and large converted by violent force under Charlemagne. Many centuries later, the Protestant Reformation brought even more bloody imposition of belief, and fiery repression of any deviation of Church approved belief to the peasantry who had to suffer and accustom themselves to these horrific impositions of thought-change. So, while remnants of indigenous worldview do linger on in obvious ways in the German tradition, and we see overt paganism in certain German folktales (such as in Vol. V of this series, Grimms' "Aschenputtel"), we can also see quite plainly that the German version of this story was heavily altered when it is compared with the Czech version; which offers a less altered, and therefore a more purely indigenous European manifestation.

It is significant that in the Czech version the hero crosses *first* across the black sea carried by the ferryman, because this represents his journey from the realm of mortals into the *Otherworld*. In native European belief, the Otherworld was not "evil," or bad in any way. The spirits of our dead loved ones often dwelled there, but it was nothing to do with punishment or a terrible fate. In the Czech tale, the ferryman takes the hero into a land of wondrous things. And he comes to cities where these wondrous things have failed to wield their magic. So, he demonstrates his good character by offering to help bring these wonders back to life.

However, in the more Christianized German version, the hero passes through these cities first *before* reaching the ferryman. Since the Christianized version changes the "Sun" into the "Devil," well, the ferryman's crossing across the dark sea takes on an entirely different meaning. Rather than taking the hero to the Otherworld of wonders, the ferryman takes the hero into the *Christian* Underworld, or Hell. This changes the meaning of everything that the hero encounters along his travels.

Aside from the ferryman at the black sea, the hero of both versions encounters kings in two cities. The first city holds a tree that once grew the "apples of youth" which would restore youth to any who ate of them. In the Czech version the apples are described with this magical property, but in the German version they are described as "golden apples," but without any special powers. Interestingly, in Norse mythology, the goddess Idunn is famous for being the guardian of the golden apples which restore youth and that is what allows the gods to be immortal. The German version remembers that the apples are golden, therefore special, but not that they held any magical powers. The hero in both versions is asked to find out why the tree stopped bearing fruit.

We discussed the concept of a journey to the Otherworld in Vol. III of this series, "Thomas the Rhymer." In that story, the hero, Thomas, travels with his guide, the Fairy Queen, where he crosses the threshold into the Otherworld. Once in that realm, he is given an apple that gives a supernatural gift to those who eat it. So, there is a parallel in the Czech version of "The Three Golden Hairs," where the hero, Plavachek, crosses the dark sea with the ferryman to the Otherworld and finds the tree with the apples of youth.

The remedy to make the trees bear fruit also differs between the two versions of this tale. In the Czech version, the Sun says that there is a snake gnawing at the roots of the tree which has caused it to stop bearing fruit. Again, we find a parallel in Norse mythology. The Norse happen to be the language group which preserved Teutonic mythology, but their overall mythos had at one time been shared by other Teutonic peoples, including the Anglo-Saxons and the Germans. And, their recorded mythology tells us that they believed in a "world tree," called Yggdrasil. In the lore, a great serpent lives at the base of the tree and gnaws on its roots. So here in the Czech version of "The Three Golden Hairs," we see the tree that bears the apples of youth is conflated with the world tree. It mimics both supernatural trees found in Germanic mythology.

Idunn and the Apples by James Doyle

Not only does the German version remove the magical properties from this tree, but the Devil tells the hero that the reason for its failure to bear golden apples is due to a mouse gnawing at its roots, not a snake. Maria Tatar, in "The Annotated Grimm," suggests that the mouse is symbolic of the Underworld, as it is a creature that dwells below ground. Granted, snakes may also represent below-earth-dwelling creatures. However, it is uncanny that the tree in the Czech version shares not one but two elements with the trees from Old Norse mythology.

In the next city, the hero learns that there is a well that has run dry. Again, in the German version, the well is special but not supernatural. In the German tale, the well once flowed with wine. But, in the Czech version, the well once flowed with the "water of life." Any person who was sick would be made well by this water, and even a dead person would be brought back to life. The belief in sacred wells and springs is rife throughout Europe. We know that these water sources were believed to have potent healing powers during the pre-Christian era. Later, the Catholic Church often built churches beside the wells, such as seen in Glastonbury, England. If not a church building, the well was often dedicated to a saint, sometimes with a small structure built over or beside it. Even to this day, people visit sacred water sources seeking healing or supernatural blessing.

So, again, it is significant that in the Czech version, the hero encounters these wonders *after* he crosses the black sea with the ferryman. Just as Thomas, in "Thomas the Rhymer," crosses into Fairy Land by going through a dark cave with an underground river and there encounters magical things, Plavachek crosses the black sea with the ferryman into the Otherworld and there encounters these supernatural occurrences. Not only are the supernatural elements removed in the German variant, but the items occur before the hero meets the ferryman, indicating he is still firmly in the land of mortals until that crossing which brings him to the realm of the devil.

It is a bit ironic that Germanic mythology is preserved in this West Slavic fairy tale when these elements are missing from the German version. However, as explained in previous chapters, there was a strong ethnic-German presence in the Czecho-Slovak region for centuries. So, the presence of Germanic myth in this tale is evidence of German cultural presence in Czech consciousness. And, of course, both language groups share Indo-European (Aryan) mytho-inheritance.

8

Baba Yaga as Ancient Goddess

The preceding chapter was not meant to suggest that "The Three Golden Hairs" is strictly a Germanic tale that wandered somehow into Slavic territory. For, there is an abundance of Slavic mythical presence in this tale. Rather, this story is a testament to the uniqueness of Czech culture to have at one time been such a hybrid of German and Slavic elements.

It was briefly mentioned above that the famous Baba Yaga appears in this tale. This is in reference to Plavachek's fairy godmother, who is also one of the Fates. To understand this connection, refer back to our discussion in Vol. V of this series on the fluidity of belief in the myth/folklore tradition. The worldview that operated in European indigenous belief was free-flowing, which can be difficult for monotheistic or atheistic-rationalist thinkers to wrap their heads around. A figure from myth, just like folktales themselves, may shift and blend, may merge into other figures, or may separate from one into two figures. One good analogy is the Norse figures of Frigg and Freyja, whom some scholars argue stem from a single goddess who later split into two. Both also may be aspects of an original proto-Indo-European (Aryan) goddess who was the source of the German Holle and Slavic Mokosh.

Most scholars agree that Baba Yaga is a figure who evolved from a very ancient goddess figure, originating as far back as the Paleolithic Era (the Old Stone Age). She often presents as an evil witch in Slavic folklore. We've discussed how, in general, Slavic folklore preserved ancient belief very strongly, but it was also not immune from the effects of Christianization. And, just as some German folktales preserve overt pagan elements (like "Aschenputtel") while others show more Christianization, of course we will see a spread on the Slavic spectrum as well. So, there are tales that present Baba Yaga as heavily demonized, but others that depict her in a more kindly and grandmotherly way.

There are many clues in this tale which point to the godmother representing Baba Yaga in addition to being referred to as one of the Fates. Firstly, just to be clear, although she is often seen in Russian tales, she does also have a Czech variation. In the Czech language, she is called *Jazi Baba*. That name is not used in this story, but there are clues that it is her.

Baba Yaga by Ivan Bilibin

In some Slavic folktales, the sun itself is said to be under the control of Baba Yaga, who can even control time and the changing of day to night. The Czech version of "The Three Golden Hairs" portrays the fairy godmother figure as the Sun figure's mother. This gets complicated, and we'll go into more of this in the next chapter. For now, it suffices to say that there is a connection and relationship between Baba Yaga and the sun. So her relationship with the Sun figure in this tale is one important clue.

As mentioned in the previous chapter, I do assert that the German conception of "the devil's grandmother" is a vestigial remnant of an ancient pagan goddess figure, demonized under a Christianized worldview. Here, Baba Yaga would also be an evolved form that was altered from an earlier goddess. But, we can see that this Czech form is closure to the source than the German idea of "the devil's grandmother," which is so removed as to be obscure and fuzzy.

Another clue that this fairy godmother is Baba Yaga is that her son, the Sun, is called "Grandfather Know-it-all" in the Czech version of "The Three Golden Hairs." Just like the German figure Frau Holle, Baba Yaga became associated with witches and witchcraft. It is very interesting that the Russian word for "witch" is *ved'ma*, which stems from the root word *ved*, meaning "to know."

In the English language, our words for both "witch" and "wizard" also evolved from the root for "to know," and are etymologically related to the word "wise." So, although the fairy godmother in this tale is not portrayed as a witch, she is associated with an anthropomorphic sun who bears the name "Know-it-all." While the godmother is not giving the hero the answers he seeks, it is clear that it was her who guided him to the Sun to find his answers.

In addition, there is reason to believe that Baba Yaga is related to the Fates. In Russian folklore, she shares many of the same roles and responsibilities that the Fates do, such as presiding over life and death, mapping out the course of an individual's life, decides the day and time of their death, and hovers over the birth of every new life.

After Christianization, we know that there was a conflating of pagan deities with Christian figures. Some were absorbed into the figures of Christian saints, some were demonized, and some goddesses had their attributes absorbed into the figure of the Virgin Mary. "The Encyclopedia of Russian and Slavic Myth and Legend," by Mike Dixon-Kennedy, says that Baba Yaga was sometimes conflated with Mother Mary. We also know that the figure of Jesus Christ absorbed elements of solar deities found throughout Europe and the Near East. So, again, the godmother portrayed as mother of the Sun hints at a Baba Yaga connection.

Saint Brigid of Kildare is the most famous example of a Catholic saint absorbing pagan iconography and attributes

Last but not least, there is one more hint that Plavachek's godmother is Baba Yaga. While this type of ancient goddess-turned-fairy-tale-figure is profoundly associated with the realm of women, the folk tradition informs us that these maternal figures loomed largely in the realm of menfolk as well. In the case of Baba Yaga, there is a tendency for her to be shown being kinder and gentler to male characters, while she is portrayed as more wicked and fearsome in tales with a female protagonist. So, the role of a maternal fairy godmother who protects and guides this young man is not at all anathema to Baba Yaga's reputation.

So, to be clear, yes, I am asserting that this godmother character in "The Three Golden Hairs" is simultaneously a traditional "fairy godmother" archetype, and one of the Fates, and Baba Yaga, and an ancient goddess. Are the Fates separate and distinct from fairy godmothers and Baba Yaga? Yes. Does that matter? No. In order to understand the fluid nature of indigenous European belief, one has to open their mind to the free-flow of thought. The Judeo-Christian paradigm views the world through a rigid, linear, black and white lens. The only alternative that has been in the Western mainstream for the past century or so is the secular atheistic-rational lens, which is again, a rigid, linear, and black and white vision. Native European worldview was not dogmatic. One figure can be many, and many can merge into one.

9

Slavic Mythical Elements

So, we've explored how the Czech social fabric once held a large German element, how that ethnic-German presence is reflected in the Teutonic mythological features that turn up in "The Three Golden Hairs." We've also discussed a little bit about the history of the Slavs, their conversion process, and how this both shunted our ability to reach the original myths while at the same time preserving Slavic myth in a more actively living way in the Slavic folk consciousness. Baba Yaga is just one figure who serves as a link betwixt ancient Slavic mythology and modern folk culture. Just as we saw glimpses of Norse (Teutonic/Germanic) mythology presented in "The Three Golden Hairs," evidence of indigenous Slavic cosmology are present as well.

We discussed the concept of a ferryman who shuttles human souls across the sea to the Otherworld as a pan-European concept, and that while the Judeo-Christian worldview sees the Underworld as a place of torment, the indigenous

European worldview saw the Underworld and the Otherworld as one and the same. It was a supernatural realm, almost like another dimension where interdimensional beings dwelled. So, passing from the human dimension into the spiritual dimension was at once both the Underworld of the dead, but also the Otherworld of spiritual beings.

The Slavs believed in this as well. There is more than one word that they used for the Under/Otherworld. Dixen-Kennedy explains in his "Encyclopedia" that *Nava, Peklo,* and *Rai* were all names for concepts of the Otherworld. He says that they may be interpreted as different sections of the Underworld which contained different attributes. Most importantly (for our purposes here), elements of the Slavic Underworld conception are depicted in "The Three Golden Hairs."

The Isle of the Dead by Arnold Böcklin

The ferryman in this story is described as rowing back and forth across a "black sea." The Underworld called *Nava* to the Slavs is also the name of the black sea that one must cross to arrive there. In addition, Baba Yaga is associated with the Underworld in several Slavic legends. As explained in the previous chapter, there is strong reason to believe that the fairy godmother in this tale is Baba Yaga, and Plavachek finds her with her son, the Sun, after he crosses the black sea. This is more indication that the character is, indeed, crossing into the Otherworld.

Even more evidence is found in the presence of the Sun figure. One of the other conceptions of the Slavic Under/Otherworld, *Rai*, is also said to be the place from whence the sun rises and sets each day. In the same way that the sun set there and was again reborn in the morning, the Slavs believed this was the place where souls went after they died and were waiting for rebirth. And, in the story, Grandfather Know-it-all, the Sun, rises and sets from his palace in the Otherworld.

But, this Sun character has even more layers of meaning. We've already discussed how the German version, in my opinion, is more removed from the original source and that the presence of "the devil" is evidence of Judeo-Christian gerrymandering of indigenous European myth. Much evidence has been laid out to support the theory that the Czech hero, Plavachek, transcends into the Otherworld, that his godmother is Baba Yaga, and that Baba Yaga is a goddess figure. Now, now for the *pièce de résistance* of this theory.

Dažbog, or Dazhbog, a Slavoc Sun God

Suggesting that this Sun figure is a pagan deity is not arbitrary conjecture. The fact that earthy and elemental imagery is rife throughout Slavic mythology has already been mentioned. But, the lynchpin is that the Slavs once had a solar deity who shared a very telling detail with this "Grandfather Know-it-all" character in "The Three Golden Hairs." In the story, the Sun starts out each day as a small child, grows into a man by noon, and by evening he returns home as an old man. Well, the Slavic solar deity, *Dazhbog*, is noted to do the exact same thing.

Curiously, this motif of the aging figure being reborn to his youth each morning is absent from the German rendition of the story. However, it is worth pointing out that dying and rising again is a common theme among solar deities. Circling back to what was mentioned in previous chapter, Baba Yaga as mother of the Sun is a parallel to the Virgin Mary as mother of Christ.

Another interesting point is that the solar god Dazhbog is said to have been also a god of blessings. It is clear in "The Three Golden Hairs" that the interaction with Grandfather Know-it-all (the Sun) is what will secure the hero, Plavachek, his destiny. And, the Sun's answers to his questions are what results in riches being granted to Plavachek as a reward. These answers also bless the people for whom Plavachek asked the questions.

So, the Sun in this tale is clearly doling out blessings.

Returning to the discussion on the German version for a moment, I want to reiterate that I do agree with Maria Tatar, editor of "The Annotated Grimm," that this story is related to "Jack in the Beanstalk"... but not in the way she thinks. (You will read that the Sun figure arrives to his home, sniffs the air, and declares that he smells the blood of a human being, reminiscent of the "fee, fie, fo, fum" scene). If anything, the insight gained from analyzing the Czech version, coupled with some other things we've learned throughout the process of developing this series, indicates that "Jack in the Beanstalk" very likely has very deep connotations that a typical reader cannot even comprehend. But *that* we will have to save for a future volume!

In any case, we have really dug deep into the world of indigenous European cosmology and spiritual belief in this volume. So, my hope is that you will find reading "The Three Golden Hairs" as exhilarating of an experience as researching it was for me.

10

"The Three Golden Hairs"

Once upon a time there was a king who loved hunting. One day while he was stalking a stag, he was led deep into the forest and became lost. When night fell, he did not know how to find his way out again. The king came upon a clearing in the woods where there was a cottage lived in by a poor woodsman and his wife. So, the king knocked on the door and told the woodsman that he would pay him a very good reward if he would lead him out of the forest.

"Of course, I would be glad to help you," said the woodsman, "but my wife is in labor with our first child right now, so I cannot leave her. Since it is too late for you to wander about the woods alone, please stay the night here with us. I will make a bed for you in the loft, and tomorrow I will guide you safely out of the forest." So, the king agreed to this and climbed up into the loft to sleep for the night.

After such a long day, the king was quite tired so he quickly fell asleep. But, he was awoken at the stroke of midnight by a strange light and sounds coming from the room below him. Peering down through the rafters, the king observed the woodsman was fast asleep, and his wife, who had fainted during childbirth, lay silently beside him. As his eyes scanned the room, he had to stifle a gasp at what he saw. For suddenly there appeared in the room an apparition. Standing above the newborn's cradle were three otherworldly women. The women appeared elderly with stark white hair, and they were dressed in flowing white gowns of gauze. Each woman held a single burning candle in her hand. And one by one they began to speak.

The first old woman said, "My gift to this boy is that he shall encounter great dangers upon his journey."

The second said, "My gift to him is that he shall face the dangers bravely, they shall do him no harm, and he will live a long life."

And, lastly, the third old woman said, "And for my give, I give him for his wife the baby daughter who is also born on this night to the very king who lies upstairs just now."

Then, when all three women blew out their candles, they disappeared! The king knew that he had just witnessed the three Fates deciding the destiny of the baby boy. They had decreed that the son of these destitute peasants would marry his daughter, and thereby inherit his kingdom. So, he lay awake the rest of the night trying to think of a way to thwart the designs of the three old Fates.

The Norns by Johannes Gehrts.

When the day finally dawned, the child began to cry in his cradle. It was then that the poor woodsman saw that his wife had died in the night. Holding his infant son he cried, "Oh, my poor little orphan! What shall I do with you now that you have no mother to nurse you?"

Seeing this as his opportunity to change fate, the king stepped in. "You have been so kind to me, let me return your charity," he lied. "Give the child to me and I'll see that he is raised in a good home. In addition, I will give you enough money so that you will live in comfort for the rest of your life."

The woodsman did not see how he could refuse, for the child would need to be fed and cared for while he had to be away from home working during each day. This seemed like a generous offer, and so he accepted the king's suggestion. The duplicitous king gleefully promised to send for the infant right away after he returned to his palace.

It was a few days journey before the king made it home to his palace. Upon arrival, he was given the joyous news that, indeed, his wife had given birth to a little girl. He asked for the day and time of her birth, and sure enough, she had been born on the same evening as the woodsman's son when he saw the Fates dictate the two children's destinies. So, instead of feeling overjoyed, a scowl came upon the king's face.

A fairy tale palace by Virginia Frances Sterrett

Quickly, he called over a servant and gave him instructions. "Here, take this money and go into the forest until you come to the clearing where the woodsman lives. Tell him this money comes from the king and assure him his child will be in safe hands. Once he hands the child over, take him to the river and drown him! Do as you are told or I will have you drowned!"

The servant did as he was told and found the woodsman at his cottage in the forest. The woodsman placed his tiny infant in a breadbasket and then exchanged his son for the money with the expectation that his son would live in comfort. The servant assured him that his child would be in safe hands and left with the baby in the breadbasket. But, when he got to the bridge to cross the river, the servant, as the king instructed him, dropped the basket with infant inside into the current below.

When the king heard that the mission had been completed he snickered and sneered, "Goodnight to you, little son-in-law that nobody wanted!" What the king never suspected was that the baby never drowned. In fact, the breadbasket held the child as comfortably as a cradle. As he floated along down the river, the water soothed the little boy softly to sleep.

Eventually, the basket floated along until it reached a river bend beside a fisherman's cottage. Seeing a basket floating down the river, the fisherman thought there might be something of value inside. So, he hopped into his small fishing boat and went after the basket. Upon retrieving it, he opened it up and peered inside to see a blessing greater than any treasure he could have imagined, for he and his wife had been wishing desperately for a child.

The fisherman fished the basket from the river – by Arthur Rackham

The fisherman brought the infant home to his wife and said, "My dear, all these years you have yearned for a little boy, and now you have one. The river has sent him to us!" The fisherman's wife was overwhelmed with joy. They named the child Plavachek, which means "a little boy who has come floating on the water."

Well, the river flowed on and on as the days rolled by. And, soon enough, Plavachek grew from a baby to a boy, and then into a very handsome young man. He was by far the best looking youth in the entire countryside.

One day, the king again road out that way without any attendants. It was quite a hot day, and the king became very thirsty. So, he stopped at the fisherman's cottage and bid him for a drink of cool water. Plavachek brought it out to the king who looked at the young man with awe. "What a fine lad you have there!" the king said to the fisherman. "Is he your own son?" the king asked.

The fisherman grinned, for he never tired of telling of the good fortune that he and his wife received when they were blessed with their river-child. "Well, he is and he isn't," and he told the king the story about how twenty years ago he had fished the breadbasket from the water. Well, the king went deathly pale before turning red with rage, for he knew immediately that Plavachek was the very same child whom he had

The wicked king lied to the fisherman – by Kay Nielsen

ordered to be drowned in the river. But, he quickly came to his senses and calmed himself in order to think fast. "Listen here," the king said to the fisherman, "I really must get a message delivered to my palace and I have no servants with me. Would your son deliver it for me? He will be well paid for his service."

The fisherman felt that a favor for the king must be yet another stroke of luck for his modest family and so he said, "But, of course, your majesty! Plavachek will be happy to serve you."

So, the king sat down and wrote a letter which he did not let the others see. The letter said "The young man who delivers this letter is an enemy and a danger to the crown! Have the guards run him through with their swords immediately! Let him be executed even before I return, this is my command." And then he folded up the letter and sealed it with his own signet ring.

Having no idea the contents of the letter, Plavachek set out on his journey for the palace. He had to go through a deep, dark forest. Somehow, he veered off the path and lost his way. Night began to fall, and without the light of day, Plavachek struggled through the bramble and the underbrush. Suddenly, an old woman appeared beneath the trees. "Plavachek, why are you alone in the woods so late at night? Where are you headed?"

Plavachek was not sure how this lady knew his name, but he was raised to show respect to his elders, so he simply answered her question. "I am carrying a letter from the king to his own palace upon his request. Can you point me to the road, good lady?"

"You'll not make it there tonight, dear boy." The old woman said kindly. "Say, why don't you come and spend the night at mine." When he looked hesitant, she reached out and gently touched his arm saying, "Plavachek, don't you know me? I'm your own godmother!"

Well, Plavachek had no memory of her at all, but he thought it must be true for how else would she have known his name? And, it was getting quite cold in the damp dark night, so a warm bed seemed like the best option. He agreed, and the two started walking together. Suddenly they came upon the prettiest little cottage Plavachek had ever seen, and it seemed to appear out of nowhere.

The two entered the cottage, and the young man felt quite at ease inside. He never knew that he had a godmother, but her home was every bit as cozy and welcoming as he had always imagined a grandmother's cottage would be, if he ever had one. So the old woman, his own godmother, made up a nice bed for him and, tired from his journey, Plavachek quickly fell fast asleep.

While he was snoozing away, the old women quietly reached into his pocket and withdrew the letter written by the sinister king. She swapped it out with another letter that appeared written in the king's own hand and sealed with his signet ring. The new letter now read, "The young man who delivers this letter is well known for his good character and handsome countenance. There is no better suitor in the land who would more deserve the hand of my fair daughter. He is destined to be my son-in-law. Have the wedding commence as quickly as possible, even before my return. This is my command."

A fairy tale cottage – by Thomas D. Murphy

So, the next day, Plavachek awoke well rested and refreshed. His godmother gave him a hearty breakfast and sent him along on his journey. He arrived at the palace later that day to deliver the letter, having never known what was in the original letter or that the letter had been changed. When he told the guards that he held a letter written by the king himself for no one's eyes but the queen, he was taken to her throne room. Plavachek had never been among such noble presence before, apart from meeting the king. But, the queen in all her regalia and in the magnificent palace was a vision of opulence that intimidated the poor peasant boy. His knees trembled as he handed the queen the letter.

The queen was very kindly, the opposite of her husband. She smiled at the young man, for she could see the goodness in his eyes, as she received the parchment. As soon as she finished reading it, she looked down again at Plavachek and smiled again warmly. At once, she called for the princess to be brought to the throne room and introduced her to her betrothed. Plavachek was stunned, and also embarrassed, as he stood there in his lowly peasants' garb beside the most beautiful women he had ever laid eyes upon. The queen saw his trepidation and placed her hand on his shoulder saying, "My dear boy, do not worry. You must have been chosen for my daughter with good reason. From this day onward you will never dress in peasants' clothes again."

Plavachek was ashamed of his clothes – by Rie Cramer

Then she had the servants take him to be dressed in finery fit for a prince. She ordered a great wedding feast to be prepared at once, and the two young people were married that very evening.

The king, of course, returned to his palace soon enough. He hurried into the throne room, eager for his wife to confirm that the pesky young man was slain as he commanded. However, when his queen saw him, her face beamed and she rushed to embrace him telling him how pleased she and their daughter were with his choice in a husband. The king wrenched his wife away from him, enraged. The queen, of course, was vexed and perplexed by her husband's reaction. "But, my darling," she said, "it was you who ordered the wedding!" she exclaimed as she thrust the letter still bearing his signet into his hand.

"This cannot be my letter!" bellowed the angry monarch. He closely examined the document and saw that the handwriting, the seal, and the paper were all exactly the same as his. Immediately he called for Plavachek to question him. And so, Plavachek explained how he travelled directly from his home to the palace, stopping only for the night with his godmother. The king needled him some more, asking him what his grandmother looked like. And, as Plavachek described her, the king knew instantly that the boy's godmother was the very same old woman whom he had seen through the floorboards of the woodsman's cabin on the night the boy was born. It was the Fate who had promised the poor woodsman's son would marry the princess, some twenty years ago.

At this point, the king did not know what to do. He realized that he could not stop fate now, for the two young people were already married. But, still, his pride could not accept that this peasant could waltz into his palace and marry his daughter so easily. So, after a moment of silence, the king looked Plavachek in the eye and said, "Well, what is done cannot be undone. But, see here, young man, you must understand that you cannot expect to marry the daughter of a king for nothing, for whomever marries my daughter will inherit my kingdom. So, if you want to remain with my daughter, must obtain a dowry fit for a princess.

This sounded reasonable enough to Plavachek, so he agreed that he would seek whatever the king demanded for a dowry. Then the king pronounced, "To remain with my daughter, you must journey to Grandfather Know-it-all and obtain three golden hairs from his very own head. Nothing less will suffice." The king was smug now, for he thought to himself that this was such an impossible task that it was just the way to dispose of this low-born peasant who he felt was unworthy to be his son-in-law.

Plavachek started on his journey – by Kay Nielsen

Well, Plavachek did not think twice. He was in love with his new bride and he would walk to the ends of the Earth to keep her. So, he kissed the princess goodbye and started off to seek her dowry. But, he had no idea what direction to travel in. Who would know where to find Grandfather Know-it-all? Everyone spoke of him, but nobody seemed to know where to find him. This was precisely what the king had been thinking. But, the king forgot one thing. Plavachek had a Fate for a godmother, so it was not likely that he would take the wrong road.

Plavachek traveled long and far, over wooded hills and desert plains. He crossed deep valleys and raging rivers. Onward he journeyed, until he found himself at a dark, black sea. At the edge of the sea he saw that a boat stood waiting, and upon it was an old ferryman. Friendly fellow that he was, Plavachek called out, "God bless you, old ferryman!"

"Thank you! May God grant that prayer, for my days are long and weary," answered the old man. "Where are you headed, young traveler?"

"I am going to old Grandfather Know-it-all to get three of his golden hairs," Plavachek answered cheerfully.

"You don't say?" replied the ferryman. "For some twenty years I have been waiting for a seeker such as yourself! For, all this time I have been ferrying people back and forth across this black sea and nobody has come to relieve me. I will ferry you to the other side if you will promise to ask Grandfather Know-it-all when my work will end."

Plavachek said that was no problem, and so the ferryman steered his vessel to the other side of the dark sea. From there, Plavachek continued on his journey. Onward he traveled, and eventually he came to a city that was in a terrible state of decay. At the city gates, he met an old man who crawled along, pulling himself along the ground with a staff. Plavachek greeted him, "God bless you, old grandfather!"

"May God grant that prayer," answered the old man, "for the whole city is in decline and I have suffered so. Tell me, handsome fellow, where do you travel?"

"I am going to old Grandfather Know-it-all to get three of his golden hairs," Plavachek again answered cheerfully.

The old man broke a grin and remarked, "Well, well! I have been waiting some time for a seeker such as you! I must bring you to the king!"

So the decrepit old man led Plavachek to his king, who was very pleased to hear of his destination. "Ah, so you are going to Grandfather Know-it-all! Excellent! Dear boy, please will you

Plavachek met a withered old man – by Kay Nielsen

help us? We have an apple tree here in this city that used to bear the apples of youth. If anyone ate just one apple, no matter how old and withered he was, he would become young again. But, alas, for twenty years now our tree has not borne any fruit at all. If you would ask Grandfather Know-it-all why the apples have stopped growing, then I will reward you handsomely." Plavachek said that he was happy to do this favor, and then he set off again on his journey.

On and on he traveled until he came to another city. Like the last city, this one was not in a very good state either. The whole city appeared to be crumbling to ruins. On the outskirts of the city, a man was crying heavy tears as he buried his father. Plavachek approached him saying, "God bless you, mournful grave-digger!"

"May God grant that prayer, kind traveler," the grave-digger replied, "where do you travel?"

And Plavachek explained, "I am going to old Grandfather Know-it-all to get three of his golden hairs."

At once, the poor grave-digger dried his eyes and began to smile. "To Grandfather Know-it-all, you say! Oh, it's only a pity you didn't come sooner, for our king has been long awaiting a seeker such as you! I must bring you to him."

So, the man brought Plavachek to the king of this city, which was in such a sorry state. And this king said to him, "You say you're going to see Grandfather Know-it-all? Please, will you do us a favor? We have a well here that used to flow with the water of life. If anyone drank of it, no matter how sick he was, he would get well. Even if he were already dead, a sprinkle of this water would bring him back to life. But, sadly, for twenty years or so our well has gone dry. If you would ask Grandfather Know-it-all how to make the well run with the water of life once again, then I will reward you handsomely." Again, Plavachek said that was happy to do this favor, and then he set off again on his journey.

Onward our young Plavachek traveled, long and far, until he came to a black forest. Deep within the dark forest he went until he came upon a clearing where there was a wide green meadow full of beautiful flowers blossoming in radiant colors. Plavachek was stunned by the beautiful view, but as he walked closer then he could not believe his eyes. Nestled in the center of the meadow appeared a golden palace that sparkled and shone as if it were on fire! He knew immediately that he had found the palace of Grandfather Know-it-all.

A sparkling palace seemed to arise from the ground – 20ᵗʰ century painting of Neuschwanstein Castle

Plavachek did feel nervous, but he had come this far. So, he walked boldly up to the entrance and was surprised to see that there were no guards. He tried the knob, and to his shock, the doors swung open. Not knowing what else to do, Plavachek slowly entered the palace, and tiptoed through the place. It appeared completely empty… and then he saw a little old lady sitting quietly at her spinning wheel in the corner. "Well, hello there, Plavachek! I'm so happy to see you again and I have been expecting you," the old woman said warmly.

Elderly woman with spinning year around the year 1900

Well, Plavachek was dumbfounded to see his godmother there! But, he found his voice and greeted her in return. "Godmother," he started, "I am here on account of the king. He says that I cannot be his son-in-law for nothing, so I must give a dowry fit for a princess, and that only three golden hairs from Grandfather Know-it-all's own head will suffice. What can I do?"

The old woman stopped her spinning, looked at her godson, and grinned brightly. "Plavachek, don't you know who Grandfather Know-it-all is? Why, he is the bright Sun! He goes everywhere and he sees everything. And, what you did not know is that I am his mother. In the morning when the day begins, my son is just a young boy. By noon he is a full grown man. And, when evening falls he has aged to an old grandfather. My dear boy, I will get you three of the golden hairs from his own golden head, or I am not a very good godmother! But, my dear, you must not remain out in the open where he can see you. My son is usually kind, but if he comes home from his day's work hungry, then he might want to roast you and have you for his supper. There is an empty tub over there. Curl up on the floor and I will turn it over you so he will not know you are here."

Plavachek did as he was told, but then he remembered the three questions that he promised to get answers about. Quickly, he lifted up the tub and told his godmother the questions. "Yes, dear," the old woman said, "I will ask my son for you, but you must listen carefully for his replies. Hush now!"

Suddenly there was the sound of a great wind, as if a tornado was outside the window! Plavachek quickly lowered the tub and remained very quiet. The Sun himself, who appeared just as she had said, as an old grandfather with a golden head, flew in by the western window. As soon as he entered he began to sniff the air suspiciously. "What is that stench?" he cried. "It smells of human flesh! Mother, do you have anyone here with you?" the old Sun demanded.

"Oh, star of the day, who could I have here without your seeing them?" she chuckled innocently. "My son, you have been flying all day long over the Earth and that is why your nose is filled with the smell of human flesh." The old man seemed satisfied at that, and sat down to have his supper.

After he had eaten his fill, the old man laid down to sleep and rested his shining golden head upon his mother's lap. Tired from a hard day's work, the Sun was soon snoring. The old woman gently pulled out a golden hair from his head and tossed it on the floor. The hair twanged like the string of a violin as it popped out of his head. The Sun awoke with a start, saying, "What is it, mother? What happened?"

Vintage illustration of a Slavic solar deity

"Nothing, my darling boy, it was nothing. I was asleep and I had a strange dream," the old woman coddled her son.

"What did you dream about, mother," asked the Sun.

"I dreamt about a city where they had a well of living water. If anyone drank from this well, no matter how sick he was, he would get better. Even if he were dead already, just a sprinkle of this water would bring him back to life. And, for the last twenty years, this well has gone dry. Is there any way to make it flow with the water of life once again?"

Yawning, the Sun answered drowsily, "Yes, mother, there is. There is a frog sitting on the spring that feeds the well. Let them kill the frog and clean out the well, and then the water of life will flow as before..." And then he drifted off back to sleep.

When he was snoring again, the old woman pulled out a second hair and threw it on the floor. Again, her son woke up saying, "What is it, mother?"

She answered him, "Nothing my dear boy, nothing. I just fell asleep again and had another strange dream. I dreamt of a city where they had an apple tree that bore the apples of youth. If anyone ate one of those apples, no matter how old they were, they would become young again. But, for

111

twenty years, the tree has borne no fruit. Can anything make the tree bear the apples of youth again?"

And, again, the Sun knew the answer. Sleepily, he answered and said, "Yes, of course. In the roots of the tree there is a snake that takes all of the tree's strength. If they would kill the snake and transplant the tree, then it will bear the apples of youth once more."

The sentence trailed off as the Sun fell back asleep again. And, for a third time, the old woman plucked a golden hair from his head and tossed it upon the floor. This time, the Sun sat straight up and exclaimed "Why won't you let me sleep, mother?!"

She reached for him and pulled him back to her lap, stroking his hair gently, she said "Now, now, my boy, lie still. I'm sorry for waking you again, but I fell fast asleep and had another very strange dream. I dreamt of a boatman on the black sea. For twenty years he has been ferrying that boat back and forth and nobody has offered to relieve him of his duty. When will he be relieved?"

Nearly talking in his sleep now, the Sun said, "Oh, but that boatman is very silly, indeed! Why doesn't he just thrust the oar into the hands of someone else and jump ashore himself? Then the other man would have to be the ferryman instead.

But, please, mother. Will you be quiet now? I must wake up very early tomorrow morning. For, these past few days, every morning I must visit the king's daughter to dry the tears she cries every night for her husband, the woodsman's son, who her father sent away to get three of my golden hairs." And with that, he drifted off to sleep.

Plavachek's wife cried for him each night – by Kay Nielsen

Plavachek, too, fell asleep curled up beneath the tub on the floor of Grandfather Know-it-all's palace. But, in the wee hours of the morn, there was again the sound of a mighty rushing wind. Peeking out from under the rim of the tub, Plavachek saw that a beautiful golden child was waking from his slumber upon the old woman's lap. It was the glorious Sun, who had, indeed, transformed back into a child over the night. The shining child said goodbye to his mother and flew out of the eastern window.

Now the old woman walked over to the tub and flipped it over to let Plavachek out. "Here are the three golden hairs for your dowry. And, if you were listening well, you also have Grandfather Know-it-all's answers to your three questions. You best start your journey back home, for your wife is overwhelmed by worry for you. And, Plavachek, dear boy, you will now have no further need of my help, so you will never see me again. Goodbye, and good luck." Overwhelmed with gratitude, Plavachek embraced his grandmother and told her that she would always be in his heart. Then, he set off to return home to his wife.

Soon enough, Plavachek arrived in the first city on his return journey. He went straight to the king there to give him Grandfather Know-it-all's answer. "Good king, I have good news for you! Have the well cleaned and kill the frog that sits on its spring. If you do this, the water will flow again as it used to."

And then the water of life flowed again – by Rie Cramer

And so, the king ordered this to be done. Immediately, the water of life began to flow once again. The king was so grateful that he gave Plavachek a very rich reward of twelve beautiful horses who were as white as swans. All twelve horses were laden with as much gold and silver as they could carry. Plavachek thanked the king for his generosity and continued on his journey.

He came to the second city and, again, asked to be taken to the king. "Good king, I have good news for you! Have the apple tree dug up. You will find a snake gnawing at its roots. Kill the snake and replant the tree, and then it will bear the apples of youth once again." And so, the king ordered this to be done. The tree was replanted at dusk, and by dawn the next morning the tree had burst into bloom with apple blossoms for the first time in twenty years. The king was so delighted that he gave Plavachek a reward of twelve horses who were as black as ravens. And, again, every horse was laden with as much treasure as it could carry.

And so, Plavachek continued his journey. He traveled on and on until he returned to the shores of the black sea. The tired ferryman's eyes lit up with hope when he saw Plavachek approaching. "Did you ask Grandfather Know-it-all my question?" he asked eagerly.

"Yes, I did," said Plavachek earnestly. "And, I will tell you the answer after you ferry me

The tree burst forth with the apples of youth – by Rie Cramer

to the other side of this black sea." The boatman pressed him for his answer, but Plavachek was very firm that he would only tell him once he was safely landed on the other side. So, the old man ferried him and his twelve white horses and twelve black horses across the dark sea.

When they had landed and Plavachek stepped onto the dry land, he said to the ferryman, "I thank you for your service, and here is your answer. The next person who comes to be ferried over, thrust your oar into his hands and quickly jump onto the shore. Then the other man will have to be the ferryman in your place." The boatman was astounded that he had never thought of this himself, and thanked Plavachek for this insight.

Finally, Plavachek made it back home to the palace of the first king and to his princess bride. The nasty old king could hardly believe his eyes when he saw the young man carrying the three long shining hairs of Grandfather Know-it-all, which sparkled and shone brightly. And, the young princess' eyes flowed with tears again with happiness at her bridegroom's return.

The king was astounded again when he saw the twelve white and twelve black horses following Plavachek, all laden heavy with immense treasure. "Where on Earth did you get these gorgeous horses and all of this wealth, Plavachek?" the king could barely gasp out the words.

*The wicked king could barely believe his eyes – by
Rie Cramer*

Plavachek held his head high and said proudly, "I have earned them on my journey." And, he told the tale of his travels.

"Apples of youth, you say! Water of life!" explained the king in wonder. And then he thought selfishly to himself "If I ate one of those apples, I would become young again! If I were dead, the water of life would restore me! And then I would never have to hand my kingdom over to this wretched peasant…" And, just like that, the wicked old king decided that he, too, would go on the very same journey.

The king set off at once to seek his own reward. And do you know what? He still has not come back! And so it was that Plavachek, the poor woodsman's son, did become the king's son-in-law just as the old Fate had divined. The queen insisted that Plavachek rule the kingdom until the king returned. But, well, as for the king… it seems he is still ferrying that boat back and forth across the black sea! And Plavachek and his princess lived happily ever after.

THE END

Plavachek and his princess lived happily ever after – by Kay Nielsen

Bibliography:

Chamberlain, Isobel Cushman. "The Devil's Grandmother." *Journal of American Folk-Lore* XIII (1900): 278-280.

Dixon-Kennedy, Mike. *Encyclopedia of Russian and Slavic Myth and Legend*. Santa Barbara: ABC-CLIO, 1998.

Fillmore, Parker. *Czechoslovak Fairy Tales*. New York: Harcourt, Brace and Company, 1919.

Fletcher, Richard. *The Barbarian Conversion: From Paganism to Christianity*. Berkeley: University of California Press, 1997.

Ivanits, Linda J. *Russian Folk Belief*. Armonk: M. E. Sharp, Inc., 1989.

Kononenko, Natalie. *Slavic Folklore: A Handbook*. Westport: Greenwood Press, 2007.

Myth and Mankind. *Forests of the Vampire: Slavic Myth*. London: Duncan Baird Publishers, 1999.

Simpson, Jacqueline. *European Mythology*. London: The Hamlyn Publishing Group, 1987.

Tatar, Maria, ed. *The Annotated Brothers Grimm*. New York: Norton & Company, Inc, 2004.

Wratislaw, A. H. *Sixty Folk Tales From Exclusively Slavonic Sources*. Cambridge: The Riverside Press, 1890.

Zipes, Jack. *The Oxford Companion to Fairy Tales*. Oxford: Oxford University Press, 2000.

About the Author:

Carolyn Emerick writes about the history, mythology, and folk belief of Northwestern Europe. She has a bachelor's degree in English literature, and possesses a lifelong learning and love of European cultural heritage.

Learn more at:

www.CarolynEmerick.com

Subscribe for $1 at:

www.Patreon.com/CarolynEmerick

Follow on Facebook at

www.Facebook.com/CarolynEmerick.writer

Printed in Germany
by Amazon Distribution
GmbH, Leipzig